EMOTIONS, MOUNTAINS AND SEAS

EMOTIONS, MOUNTAINS AND SEAS

Echoes of the heart across nature's vastness

AMY LEE

Amy Lee
Emotions, Mountains And Seas
Echoes of the heart across nature's vastness

Published by Spines Publishing Platform
ISBN: 979-8-89691-214-9

CONTENTS

Part One
PROLOGUE: THE OVERTURE OF MOUNTAINS AND SEAS

1. The First Greeting of Mountains and Seas — 3
2. Spring Breeze Knocks — 4
3. The Rise of the Tide — 6
4. The First Sunlight Pierces the Clouds — 8
5. A Prayer Between Mountains and Seas — 9

Part Two
SPRING: PRELUDE TO AWAKENING

6. Dewdrops Like Tears — 13
7. Buds Breaking the Soil — 14
8. The First Bloom of Flowers — 15
9. Whispers of the East Wind — 16
10. First Love in the Valley — 17
11. Sunlight Across the Fields — 18
12. The Invitation of Fresh Green — 20
13. Ripples of Emotion — 21
14. Waves Against the Shore — 22
15. The Swallow's Journey Home — 23
16. The Whisper of Spring Rain — 24
17. The Oath of Sprouts — 25
18. The Gentle Sway of Flower Shadows — 26
19. The Whisper of Greenery — 27
20. Dreams Shattered by Spring Wind — 28
21. The Embrace of Dawn — 29
22. The Flutter of New Life — 30
23. The Murmur in the Forest — 31
24. Dew on the Tips of Grass — 32
25. The Brook's Murmur — 34
26. The Scent of Earth — 35
27. The Willow's Whispers — 36
28. The Butterfly's First Dance — 37

29. Spring's Gentle Words ... 39
30. Confession of the Breeze ... 40
31. Whispers in the Rain ... 41
32. The Smile of Wildflowers ... 43
33. The Arrival of Warm Sunlight ... 44
34. The Beauty of Distant Mountains ... 45
35. Fields of Hope ... 47
36. The Tenderness of Moss ... 49
37. The Awakening of the Earth ... 50
38. The Whispers of the Spring Fields ... 51
39. A Feast of Fresh Green ... 52
40. The Murmur of Tender Grass ... 54
41. Branches Kissed by Morning Light ... 55
42. The Voyage of All Things ... 57
43. The Wind's Unspoken Thoughts ... 58
44. The Path's First Visitors ... 60
45. Prelude of Love ... 61

Part Three
SUMMER: PASSION IN FULL BLOOM

46. Burning Heart Beneath the Blazing Sun ... 65
47. Running Under the Scorching Sun ... 66
48. Shadows of Green Mountains ... 67
49. Summer's Whisper ... 68
50. Love Like a Blazing Flame ... 69
51. The Passion of the Tides ... 70
52. A Sky Full of Stars ... 72
53. A Midsummer Night's Dream ... 74
54. The Smiling Sunflower ... 75
55. The Storm Within the Heart ... 76
56. The Feast of Sunshine ... 78
57. The Season of Blazing Flames ... 79
58. Heatwaves Embrace the Earth ... 81
59. The Summer Dream of the Lake ... 82
60. The Fiery Promise ... 84
61. The Evening Breeze's Whisper ... 86
62. The Rhapsody of Midsummer ... 87
63. The Burning Green Canopy ... 88
64. The Blazing Years ... 89

65. The Surge of Love   90
66. The Song of the Scorching Sun   91
67. Clouds Dyed Red with Passion   92
68. Footprints on the Sand   94
69. The Fireworks of Midsummer   95
70. The Fiery Chase   96
71. The Midnight Stars   98
72. Heatwaves in the Valley   99
73. The Blazing Bagpipe   101
74. The Passionate Coast   102
75. Love Amid the Cicadas' Song   103
76. Crimson Longing   104
77. Confession of a Summer Night   105
78. Shadows Under the Scorching Sun   106
79. Youth Written in Sweat   107
80. The Burning Wheat Field   108
81. The Moth in the Flame   109
82. The Frenzy of Midsummer   110
83. Dancing in the Heatwave   111
84. The Kiss in the Fire   112
85. Chasing the Footsteps of Summer   113

Part Four
AUTUMN: WHISPER OF ABUNDANCE

86. Yellow Leaves Dancing in the Wind   117
87. Autumn Waters and Endless Skies   118
88. The Bowing Rice Stalks   119
89. The Golden Woods   120
90. The Fragrance of Memories   121
91. The Sunset's Afterglow   122
92. The Silence of Mountains and Seas   123
93. The Emotions of Red Maple   125
94. The Embers of Love   126
95. Starlight Guides the Lonely Boat   127
96. The Whisper of Autumn Wind   128
97. Golden Reflection   129
98. The Love Song of Withered Leaves   130
99. The Afterglow in the Mountains   131
100. The Poem of Autumn Days   132

101. Amber Memories   134
102. Thoughts in the Wind   135
103. The Silence of Frosted Mornings   136
104. The Tale of Autumn Leaves   137
105. The Autumn Melody of Distant Mountains   138
106. The Returning Swallow   139
107. Orange and Yellow Dreams   140
108. The Harvested Fruits of Autumn   141
109. The Journey of the Solitary Goose   142
110. Deep Thought of Golden Autumn   144
111. The Withered Branches Under Moonlight   145
112. Autumn Waters Meet the Endless Sky   146
113. The Silence of the Valley   147
114. The Deep Autumn Sentiment   148
115. The Promise of Red Leaves   150
116. The Residual Warmth of Autumn Nights   151
117. Falling Leaves Returning to the Roots   153
118. The Echoes in the Autumn Wind   155
119. The Fragrance of Fruits   156
120. The Long Thoughts of Autumn Days   157

Part Five
WINTER: ECHOES OF SERENITY

121. White Snow Draped Over Mountains   161
122. Thoughts in the Cold Wind   162
123. Stars in the Silent Night   163
124. The Frozen Sea   164
125. A Song of the Cold Moon   166
126. Disappearing Footprints   167
127. The Watchful Pine   168
128. The Bloom of Winter Plum   169
129. The Finale of Life   170
130. The Other Side of the Starry Sea   171
131. Whispers of Frost   172
132. Lonely Shadow on the Snowfield   173
133. Murmurs of the Winter Day   175
134. Vigil of the White Night   176
135. The Flow of the Ice River   177
136. Winter Sun's Greeting   178

137. Contemplation Under the Hoarfrost 179
138. Memories on the Snowfield 180
139. The Silent Glacier 182
140. Echoes of the Winter Night 183
141. The Silent Plain 184
142. The Breath of Frozen Earth 185
143. The Deep Affection of Falling Snow 186
144. A Winter Day's Sketch 187
145. The Frozen Valley 188
146. The Farewell of Frosted Leaves 189
147. A Silent Night 190
148. The Lonely Boat in the Snow 191
149. Cold Dreams 192
150. The Winter Wind's Elegy 193
151. The Deep Slumber of Bitter Winter 194
152. Snow Traces Under the Moonlight 196
153. The Whisper of the North Wind 197
154. Starlight on a Snowy Night 198
155. Eternity in Ice and Snow 199

Part Six
EPILOGUE: EMOTIONS AND THE MOUNTAINS AND SEAS

The Everlasting Mountains and Seas 203
The Farewell of the Tides 205
The Cycle of the Seasons 207
Returning to Silence 209
The Eternity of Emotions 211

Part One

PROLOGUE: THE OVERTURE OF MOUNTAINS AND SEAS

Sets the theme, unveils the poetry collection, showcasing the grandeur and deep affection of mountains and seas.

THE FIRST GREETING OF MOUNTAINS AND SEAS

Dawn lifts the veil of gentle clouds, Mountains stretch their slumbering boughs. The wind strums the brook's soft strings, A first greeting echoes where horizons cling.

The mountains murmur, telling timeless tales, The sea's longing never wanes or pales. Pine waves carry a fragrant thrill, Like a first meeting, the heart won't stay still.

Silent is the sky as mountains and seas gaze, Cradling all, where poetry finds its place. This greeting, as dreamlike as it seems, Awakens the world to dawn's golden beams.

SPRING BREEZE KNOCKS

The morning light spills over the mountains. The spring breeze gently knocks on silent doors. It awakens the slumbering buds, Blossoms embracing new hopes once more.

The breeze carries the scent of the earth, As streams sing of winter's retreat. Peach blossoms bow, willows sway, New green revives in the wind's soft heat.

The spring breeze asks, "Shall a new story unfold?" It gently pushes the doors ajar, and life overflows. Its whispers form a heartfelt prelude, Spreading radiant love across the world below.

THE RISE OF THE TIDE

The night recedes, the stars gently quiver. The tide whispers in the sea's ear. Like a dream, the sound of water wakes the shore, Waves lifted the morning's delicate sail once more.

As the tide rises, the heart beats loudly. Each crash on the rocks was tender yet proud. The moon's fading glow scatters over the waves, Draping the sea in a silvered embrace.

This is both a beginning and a return. The tide brings back old stories to be relearned. It slips away quietly, leaving its affection, Etching ancient verses along the shore's reflection.

THE FIRST SUNLIGHT PIERCES THE CLOUDS

The wind parts the veil of soft clouds. The first sunlight leaps out like a child. Golden rays spill upon the mountain crest, Waking streams and fields from their rest.

Birds cut through the morning sky with flight, Dewdrops glisten, reflecting pure light. The sun kisses every corner of the earth, Igniting all things with fervent rebirth.

Steady yet gentle, it shines with resolve, Piercing the dark, making hope evolve. In the instant sunlight pierces the sky, The world renews, and all things are revived.

A PRAYER BETWEEN MOUNTAINS AND SEAS

The mountain's silhouette is a silent song, The sea's vast embrace, deep and strong. In the morning mist, they gaze and connect, Singing an eternal hymn of respect.

The pine's rustle is the mountain's whisper, The waves' rhythm is the sea's murmur. The wind carries these silent prayers, Through the world, up to celestial layers.

The mountain prays for the earth's abundance to stay, The sea hopes life's brilliance never fades away. Together, they watch, silent but sincere, Cradling all in an endless sphere of peace.

Part Two

SPRING: PRELUDE TO AWAKENING

The vitality and hope of spring reflect the beginnings of life and the budding of emotions

DEWDROPS LIKE TEARS

Morning dewdrops fall gently, Like tear trails slipping across blades of grass. The earth awakens in the break of dawn, Each drop whispers profound emotions.

They reflect the vastness of the sky, Yet hide the night's final sorrow. The breeze caresses them, and they silently fall, Weaving fleeting blossoms with the sunlight.

Though brief, dewdrops are dazzling, Like fleeting yet precious scenes in life. They vanish quietly in the morning glow, Leaving memories eternal within the heart.

BUDS BREAKING THE SOIL

A hint of fresh green peeks through the soil, Breaking winter's grip with steadfast resolve. The gentle breeze brings a warm touch, Uplifting the earth's first breath of spring.

Its stem is tender, its roots still small, Yet it proudly reaches for the sunlight. It knows the soil's nurturing embrace, And hears the spring rain's whispers.

Though voiceless, the sprout's power is profound, A symbol of life's earliest promise. Each emergence is a hymn of rebirth, Singing spring's endless perseverance.

THE FIRST BLOOM OF FLOWERS

A soft breeze coaxes the buds to unfold. Their first bloom sets spring's passion ablaze. Blush pinks and soft yellows emerge, Weaving vibrant tapestries across the land.

Bees and butterflies linger nearby, Praising the flowers in their lively stage. Sunlight dances, casting golden rays, Illuminating each petal's dreams.

Though fleeting, the bloom is divine, Marking the opening chapter of spring. Its fragrance drifts far and wide, Etching beauty into every heart.

WHISPERS OF THE EAST WIND

The east wind glides over the hills, Its whispers cradling the warmth of the sun. It soothes the earth's lingering chill, Awakening the slumber of grass and trees.

Carrying floral scents across the fields, It bears life's vitality through the seasons. Every touch is tender and full of grace, Like a mother's hand, gentle and warm.

Though invisible, the east wind stirs the soul, Igniting emotions deep within. In this tranquil spring morning, It speaks of spring's eternal promise.

FIRST LOVE IN THE VALLEY

The valley is quiet; grasses sway gently. The first spring breeze stirs the heart. A murmuring brook sings of affection, Echoing the familiar pulse of first love.

A tiny flower sways at the foot of the hill, Waiting patiently, sketching a tender bond. Sunlight descends, cloaking it in radiance, Lifting it from its modest station.

First love blooms like this shy flower, Awkward yet glowing with beauty. It belongs to the valley, to spring, And to every heart that beats anew.

SUNLIGHT ACROSS THE FIELDS

Sunlight pours over the boundless fields, Bathing every inch in golden hues. Grass stretches, wheat waves roll, Shadows and light weave boundless poetry.

Distant hills wear a veil of mist. Nearby streams shimmer with brilliance. The breeze carries wafts of fragrance, Joining bird songs in a springtime symphony.

This field nurtures the seeds of hope, Flourishing under the sun's embrace. With vast and generous arms, It welcomes all who cherish life.

THE INVITATION OF FRESH GREEN

A sprig of fresh green waves from afar, Inviting us into spring's gentle embrace. Tree branches sway, grass blades dance, Blessings bestowed by the earth to all.

Treading softly, the scent of soil greets us. The sights filling the heart with poetry. That fresh green is like a childhood smile, Bringing pure laughter and trust.

It beckons us to pause and feel, The sincerity and warmth of nature. In this moment, the world is boundless, And fresh green renews life's splendor.

RIPPLES OF EMOTION

The breeze stirs, the lake ripples softly, Heartfelt tremors sway like a dreamy dance. Reflections in the water slowly disperse, Fragments of memories scatter within.

These ripples are tender yet profound, Stirring emotions deeply concealed. Without roaring waves or crashing tides, They silently tell stories of longing.

Each ripple marks a heartbeat's imprint, Leaving traces in the stream of time. The lake is voiceless but filled with affection, Its ripples carry the weight of the past.

WAVES AGAINST THE SHORE

Waves crash, tossing white foam ashore. Their voices were deep yet brimming with longing. Every surge a passionate confession, Telling the shore of an eternal yearning.

Sea breezes accompany their lively dance, Carrying the ocean's heart to distant lands. Though they come and go without rest, Their love-filled melody never ceases.

The waves' persistence moves the heart, Their relentless rhythm inspires gratitude. Along this boundless shoreline, Their cadence flows like a timeless poem.

THE SWALLOW'S JOURNEY HOME

Swallows return, harbingers of spring. Their silhouettes pierce the morning mist. Flying home from distant southern lands, They bring hope and light to the earth.

They skim rivers and crest hills, Drawing arcs of joy across the sky. A crisp call pierces the stillness, Infusing Spring with vibrant life.

With wings, they trace their love's path, Their resolve a stirring testament. The eaves of home await faithfully, Swallows' return, spring's finest ribbon.

THE WHISPER OF SPRING RAIN

Gentle rain taps softly on the windowpane. Its whispers scatter across the springtime sky. Droplets fall on branches, waking fresh green;They seep into the soil, nurturing Earth's dreams.

The rain's melody is like soft murmurs, Telling tales of rebirth and tender emotion. Each droplet carries a seed of hope, Quietly growing in spring's warm embrace.

Though silent, the rain speaks volumes-A gift of the seasons, a prelude to life. It whispers its message, and the world listens:Spring's future begins with this moment.

THE OATH OF SPROUTS

Sprouts break through the soil with youthful vigor. Their life pledge shines under the sun. Each tender leaf is a promise of courage, A vow to face the future with hope.

The wind caresses their fragile faces. The rain nourishes their growing hearts. Though frost and trials lie ahead, They march forward, undaunted by fear.

The oath of sprouts is nature's confession, And life's eternal anticipation. From this day, hope rises with the earth, A new chapter begins in life's story.

THE GENTLE SWAY OF FLOWER SHADOWS

Sunlight pours down, and flower shadows sway. Every blossom carries the smile of spring. The breeze lifts fragile stems in its arms, Painting the earth with vibrant colors.

Shadows dance gracefully in the golden light, Whispering tales of time's tender journey. Fragrance adorns the passing days, Writing verses of beauty in the seasons.

Within the swaying lies life-deep affection, Each movement reveals spring's pure intention. Though fleeting, the flower shadows leaveEternal warmth is etched in the heart of the earth.

THE WHISPER OF GREENERY

Green creeps quietly over the hills;Spring whispers softly through tender leaves. In the breeze, they murmur secrets of renewal, Telling the story of the earth's awakening.

Each leaf brims with promise and hope, Composing melodies of vibrant life. They carry the caress of sunlight, Delivering optimism deep into the soil.

Hushed yet powerful, green voices call, Reviving the world with their gentle touch. This quiet plea breathes life into spring, A hymn of gratitude to existence.

DREAMS SHATTERED BY SPRING WIND

Spring wind drifts through the valleys, Shattering the remnants of winter's dreams. It sweeps away solitude and frost, Clothing the earth in a fresh new guise.

Every gust is a messenger of life, Every whisper wakes slumbering branches. It scatters hope across the plains, Weaving warmth into the fabric of spring.

Broken dreams dissolve into dust, Melding with the earth as roots of rebirth. The spring wind, silent yet soulful, Brings renewal, healing scars of the past.

THE EMBRACE OF DAWN

Dawn wraps its arms around the earth, Golden threads of light, soft and tender. Its glow ignites the world's vast hopes, Warming all that yearns for new beginnings.

Dew sparkles on the tips of leaves. Birdsong fills the air with joyful praise. Dawn, though silent, brims with love, Its embrace stirs life from peaceful slumber.

This gentle hold, like a mother's care, It brings a sense of calm to all it touches. As dawn appears, dreams fade, Unveiling a world freshly alive with promise.

Young shoots peek timidly from the earth. Heartbeats quicken with the thrill of rebirth. Each fresh green leaf conveys courage, Every breeze cradles their breath of life.

Spring arrives on quiet, soft footsteps, Awakening all from their wintry rest. They stretch towards the warm sunlight, And murmur their thanks in gentle whispers.

The flutter of new life declares its arrival, Nature's hymn for the days to come. This earth has never felt so alive, It's every corner glows with love's energy.

THE MURMUR IN THE FOREST

In the forest, faint sounds softly rise—The wind's gentle whispers, trees' quiet sighs. They wander through sunlit and shadowed glades, Telling stories of nature's most profound hopes.

Streams babble in harmony with birdsong. Leaves rustle, a chorus of light and shadow. The forest's murmurs are spring's secret voice, A tender melody of rebirth and grace.

Every corner brims with promise anew, Every patch of green reaches higher. The forest's murmur holds endless devotion, A vow of life's unyielding emotion.

DEW ON THE TIPS OF GRASS

Dewdrops gleam on the tips of the grass, Glittering under the morning's first light. A night of dreams evaporates into the air, Leaving a moment of fleeting brilliance.

Each dewdrop carries greetings from the sky, Reflecting the earth's unspoken tenderness. Though brief, they shine with infinite worth, Embodiments of life's purest essence.

A gentle breeze coaxes them to glide away, Taking with them whispers of the night. Slender grass cradles these drops of hope, Glowing at the dawn of each new day.

THE BROOK'S MURMUR

Deep in the valley, the brook softly hums, Gently caressing rocks, its song quietly strums. Each flowing moment plucks nature's strings, Echoing tenderness with serene swings.

By the brook, flowers shyly unfold, Their reflections in the waters boldly glow. The sparkling ripples scatter time's essence, A fleeting beauty turns into an eternal presence.

It carries fallen leaves and stories untold. Past moments seep into earth's gentle hold. Each droplet bears a dream's endeavor, Rushing forward, seeking forever.

THE SCENT OF EARTH

After morning rain, the earth releases its scent, A dream of soil, deep and unbent. It holds seeds' promises and their yearning, Whispering cycles of time, ever turning.

Each inch of soil cradles life's grace, Every grain, steadfast warmth in place. It embraces roots, nurturing green, Composing a melody in nature's serene.

This fragrance is the heartbeat of the world, Born for renewal, into future hurled. It tells us that hope never fades away, The earth's arms cradle loves each day.

THE WILLOW'S WHISPERS

A gentle breeze strokes drooping willows, Their murmurs weave tales, soft and mellow. Branches sway like tender verses, In spring sunlight, they sing life's purpose.

The lake mirrors the willows' silhouette, Swaying quietly with unspoken depth. Leaves strum spring's delicate tune, Each tremble responds to the heart's croon.

The willow whispers, like time's caress, Accompanying rivers through dawns and darkness. No matter how storms fiercely lash, They stand steadfast, whispers never dashed.

THE BUTTERFLY'S FIRST DANCE

Dawn arrives, dewdrops gleam, Butterflies spread wings and vivid dreams. In flowers' embrace, they softly soar, Spring's melody flows, gentle once more.

Every flutter praises life's fire, Each pause whispers of hope's desire. Short but intense, they spend their flight, Etching poems in earth's sunlight.

The butterfly's dance is nature's prelude, Soft yet firm, its trail imbued. Though colors fade, their steps remain, Imprinted forever on the heart's domain.

SPRING'S GENTLE WORDS

Spring breezes sweep, branches lightly sway, Spring's murmurs softly echo away. Grass blades peek, fields turn green, A breath of warmth wakes slumbering scenes.

Streams babble through mountain bends, Buds shyly bloom and smiles ascend. These gentle whispers greet spring's birth, Planting hope deep in earth's mirth.

Every breeze carries a tender plea, Every inch of land awaits jubilee. Spring speaks without words yet declares, New life awaits, and the world repairs.

CONFESSION OF THE BREEZE

A soft breeze stirs, brushing the plains. Its whispers reveal gentle refrains. Carrying flowers' scents and silent thoughts, It murmurs what time never forgot.

Gliding over hills, through bubbling streams, In the woods, it joins birds' tranquil themes. Its confessions are silent yet profound, Touch each leaf, making hearts resound.

The breeze declares sweet devotion. Across four seasons, love's proper motion. Each quiet dawn and hushed twilight, It guards nature's secrets, pure and bright.

WHISPERS IN THE RAIN

Raindrops like silk gently kiss the earth, Their whispers sing spring's rebirth. Pitter-patter taps against the windowpane, Softly recounting hopes born of rain.

They settle on leaves, nurture green, Sink into the soil, crafting life unseen. Though small, the rain exudes strength, Scattering hope across the land's length.

Each drop speaks of love's silent embrace, Each murmur fills hearts with grace. The rain brings peace, a thoughtful hymn, Awakening earth, letting life begin.

THE SMILE OF WILDFLOWERS

Deep in valleys, spring breezes entwine. The first wildflower offers its shy smile. It blooms humbly, quietly serene, Brightening the silent mountainside scene.

Soft petals, colors ablaze, Reflect dreams in earth's still gaze. Every waft of fragrance carries hope, Sweeping away winter's shadowy cloak.

Wildflowers, heralds of springtime's cheer, Smile brightly in verses sincere. Though their time is fleeting and brief, Their beauty gifts the earth relief.

THE ARRIVAL OF WARM SUNLIGHT

Dawn breaks; warm sunlight spills. Its glow blankets valleys and hills. Its embrace, like a mother's care, Kindles the world with renewal rare.

Dewdrops shimmer, slipping to the ground. Light dances gently, spreading around. It wakes slumbering life anew, Stirring hearts with affection is genuine.

Warm sunlight's arrival, a ritual profound, Infusing the day with poetry unbound. Symbol of hope, beacon of life, Guiding us toward a future.

THE BEAUTY OF DISTANT MOUNTAINS

Draped in spring's gauzy veil, Distant mountains reveal their tale. They stand silently, gazing afar, Stories etched by time, profound and bizarre.

Verdant forests, brimming with sighs, Life murmurs in their heights. Streams laugh through hills below, Birdsong lingers where breezes flow.

Distant mountains, poems of the land, Every line holds nature's hand. They watch spring's gentle flight, Reflecting a world bathed in light.

FIELDS OF HOPE

The vast field brims with vitality, Green surges forth like waves of the sea. Spring breezes bring whispers of tender, Spreading hope to every field's corner.

Grass stands tall, flowers ablaze. In sunlight's glow, life's fervor sways. Together, they sing life's praise, A chorus echoing through endless days.

Hope gallops across the plains, Its quiet power cleanses the stains. From here begins a journey of bold, A field of hope and dreams untold.

THE TENDERNESS OF MOSS

Deep in the cracks, moss quietly grows. Its tenderness is as profound as a poem flows. Each touch of green carries warmth inside, Writing the memory of years through frost and tide.

Clinging tightly to the earth, it silently stays, Nurturing hope, never retreating from its ways. Small but resilient, tender yet firm, It adds calm warmth to a world so long.

The tenderness of moss is silent yet endless, Like the earth's soft breath, serene and boundless. It whispers nature's unspoken vow, Living alongside all, eternal somehow.

THE AWAKENING OF THE EARTH

A beam of dawn spreads across the hills. The earth awakens as life refills. Tender buds sprout, green stretches far, Streams murmur as spring writes its overture.

Birdsong breaks the silence of the mist. Petals tremble, embracing spring's bliss. The wind stirs fields, rippling waves of wheat, New life's fragrance fills hearts, sweet.

Every inch of soil stretches in delight, Every flower bud harbors its light. The earth responds with passion and grace, Spring has arrived, and the future takes its place.

THE WHISPERS OF THE SPRING FIELDS

The spring fields stretch like painted dreams, Green grass blankets hills in gentle streams. When the breeze sweeps by, it whispers low, Revealing secrets only spring can know.

Butterflies chase fragrant, fleeting dreams, While flowing, Brooks sings of spring's esteem. Flowers stand still, sharing silent tales, The birds above detail nature's scales.

Each leaf is a promise of hope anew, Growing boundless under the sky's view. Spring fields cradle life's tender croon, With whispers soft as the silver moon.

A FEAST OF FRESH GREEN

Early spring arrives with a quiet grace, A feast of green spreads across nature's embrace. Treetops don a new green glow, Grass blades dance as breezes blow.

Streams run freely, brimming with glee, Their mirrors reflect the green spree. Flower buds smile, gently unfurling their hue, Life's canvas unfolds in shades so true.

This green feast declares spring's arrival, Reviving Earth from its silent survival. We immerse ourselves, marveling at the scene, Feeling every beat of life newly green.

A Feast of Fresh Green

THE MURMUR OF TENDER GRASS

Tender grass rises, quietly murmuring low, Singing spring's innocence in winds that blow. Each blade stretches toward the sun's rays, Echoing earth's heartbeat in subtle displays.

Dew rests softly on their fragile tips, As if whispering warmth to spring's lips. Roots bury deep, clasping the earth's hold, Injecting life's flow into soils bold.

This murmur is silent yet deeply felt, Waking all with its resonant belt. Though minor, tender grass holds excellent might, Murmuring timeless songs of light.

BRANCHES KISSED BY MORNING LIGHT

Morning light drapes over the waking trees. Dew sparkles like gems in the gentle breeze. Winds caress softly, with a tender touch, Bestowing hopes new to cherish much.

Flower buds bloom in the early sun, Leaves sway gently, a new day begun. Sunlight streams through the spaces of the trees, Painting shadows with poetic ease.

These branches cradle dreams in their embrace, Voicing strength with the morning's grace. Each dawn is a chance to start afresh, Embracing nature, leaving past regrets.

THE VOYAGE OF ALL THINGS

Spring winds blow softly, stirring the ground. All things set sail, new journeys abound. Seeds break the soil, reaching for light, Waters rush forth, singing life's flight.

Branches stretch wide, welcoming return. Petals bloom bright as bees' love burns. Every cloud reflects the sky's gentle gaze, Every sunbeam delivers spring's praise.

The voyage ahead is entirely unknown, Yet hearts march forward, fears overthrown. All things embark with renewed resolve, Toward futures bright, where mysteries evolve.

THE WIND'S UNSPOKEN THOUGHTS

Spring breezes sweep across the hills, Their whispers are laden with quiet thrills. They brush past flowers, then drift away, Seeking fragments of time led astray.

They ripple lakes, stirring the glassy sheen, And rustle trees with touches of serenity. The wind's thoughts are traceless and free, Yet the earth hears its silent plea.

Perhaps it tells of life's fleeting tale, Or weaves unspoken verses in its trail. No matter its story, its tender sigh, It touches hearts as it sweeps by.

THE PATH'S FIRST VISITORS

The morning path lies quiet and still, Its first visitor, the breeze, roams at will. It stirs the dew, waking their dance, Letting them glimmer in spring's chance.

Steps soon follow, lively and light, As flowers sway gently in delight. Birdsong fills the forest's frame, Enhancing the path's peaceful name.

Each visitor brings hope and cheer, Walking the path with spirits clear. This path cradles dreams in spring's glow, Stretching far where possibilities flow.

PRELUDE OF LOVE

Spring composes a melody of care, Each bird's song reveals love's flair. Streams murmur, soft and true, While breezes caress with a gentle hue.

Blossoms bloom, painting the scene. Butterflies twirl in serene dances. Life awakens, brimming with grace, Love's prelude echoes across every space.

This melody lingers, warm and strong, Etched in leaves, resonating long. Love's seeds scatter through earth and air, Its quiet power is eternal and rare.

Part Three

SUMMER: PASSION IN FULL BLOOM

The intensity and warmth of summer mirror the peak of life and the fervor of love

BURNING HEART BENEATH THE BLAZING SUN

The blazing sun scorches both the earth and the heart. Heatwaves roll, igniting hidden flames. Every ray of sunlight pierces life's branches, Lighting unburnt sparks of buried dreams.

Sweat trickles, speaking of steadfast belief. Heavy steps persist, never halting in despair. Beneath the sun, the heart blazes like fire, Turning every fleeting moment into eternal brilliance.

Even if the sky burns into a golden-red canvas, It cannot halt the strides of a fervent soul. The burning heart is not just the essence of life, But the eternal pursuit of unwavering faith.

RUNNING UNDER THE SCORCHING SUN

Sunlight paves the road ahead. Each step is forged by relentless heat. The wind whistles past my ears, Singing of freedom and the thrill of speed.

The path stretches endlessly before my feet. Sweat bears witness to dreams gone wild. Though the sun is merciless, my passion never wanes, In the run, we forge a bond with tomorrow.

This chase is not about victory or rank, But about testing our limits and our truth. Running under the scorching sun burns our passion, Letting youthful spirits shine with brilliance.

SHADOWS OF GREEN MOUNTAINS

Mountains stretch, bathed in golden light, Emerald shadows sway, casting life's glow. The wind brushes gently through the valleys, Bringing whispers of streams and birds in symphony.

Every green leaf glimmers with hope. Every mountain shadow hides a dream. The mountains are a painting, time is its brush, Writing eternal legends upon the canvas of years.

Whether in sunrise or twilight's glow, The mountains' charm flows deeply through the soul. Shadows of green mountains, eternal and vivid, The immortal poem of nature's beauty.

SUMMER'S WHISPER

The breeze caresses treetops and lakes, Summer whispers hide within cicada songs. It speaks of sunshine's warmth and fervor, And of night's calm and profound depth.

Each gust carries a secret confession, Each leaf records an era of passion. Summer's whispers are silent, Yet they seep into every dawn and dusk.

They guide us forward to distant lands, Chasing endless dreams under the sun. These unseen whispers, fleeting yet deep, Etched forever in every ardent heart.

LOVE LIKE A BLAZING FLAME

Love is a flame that scorches the soul. Its radiant light dispels every cold shadow. It sweeps through ordinary days and years, Igniting sparks within our gazes.

Though fierce, the fire brings a warm reliance, Connecting lonely hearts into a vast ocean. Love that blooms within fire is so pure, Unafraid of pain or the storms to come.

Love, like a blazing flame, is fleeting but intense. Even in ashes, there is no regret. In its glow, we embrace truth, Not distant, indifferent stars.

THE PASSION OF THE TIDES

Tides surge, their passion like rolling waves, Crashing upon rocks and human hearts. They arrive from afar, carrying the unknown, Scattering the sea's secrets across heaven and earth.

The roar of tides thunders with life's desire. The song of the sea wind points to freedom. Standing by the shore, feeling the kiss of the waves, Is nature's and humanity's shared resonance?

Even when tides recede, their mark remains, Imprinted as eternal footprints in the sand. The passion of the tides is summer's revelry, Turning the mundane into moments of brilliance.

A SKY FULL OF STARS

The night sky is deep, with stars scattered wide, Like countless hearts shining in the dark. Every star tells a story, Crossing light-years to bring warmth to Earth.

Moonlight drapes the land in a silver veil, While starlight illuminates distant horizons. They are silent yet dazzling bright, Adorning countless dreams in the night.

A sky full of stars is more than decoration, It's a vessel of yearning and poetic thought. Under the starlit expanse, we find ourselves, Tiny yet shining with the universe.

A MIDSUMMER NIGHT'S DREAM

A midsummer's night, dreamlike and hazy. The breeze brushes gently, and trees whisper faintly. Moonlight streams through forest trails, Blending the boundary of dreams and reality.

The nightingale's song echoes nearby, As if voicing a mysterious longing. Starlight reflects the shadows of the soul, Drawing one into the intoxication of the moment.

A midsummer night's dream, as fiery as it is soft, Filling the heart with water-like calm. When darkness fades, and the dream recedes, Memories linger, as eternal as starlight.

THE SMILING SUNFLOWER

Sunflowers gaze at the golden sun, Their smiles greet every ray of light. Standing tall amidst heatwaves unafraid, They chase after the sun's brilliant glory.

Their blooms blaze like miniature suns. Every petal carries the weight of hope. The wind stirs, creating waves of gold, As if the earth itself is laughing and singing.

The sunflower's smile is not fleeting, But a tribute to life's fervent passion. They teach us to face storms with joy, Greeting every day with love and light.

THE STORM WITHIN THE HEART

The heart is a storm, waves ever-churning. Heat and calm intersect in fleeting moments. Each beat echoes like thunder's roar, Driving dreams to traverse the skies.

Passion, like a hurricane, tears through the mundane, Breaking every barrier in its path. Yet peace, like post-storm breezes, Washes away confusion and sorrow within.

This storm will pass, leaving behind clarity. Traces of resilience are carved into the soul. The storm within the heart need not be feared, It is the baptism of growth and transformation.

THE FEAST OF SUNSHINE

Sunlight bathes every branch and leaf, Golden glimmers flow innocently between trees. Every green leaf, like a lifted goblet, Holds the sweet nectar bestowed by nature.

Flowers bloom with smiles in the light. Bees and butterflies busy themselves for the feast. A gentle breeze carries sunlight's greetings, Adding tenderness to the vast expanse.

The bears it all with its wide embrace. This grand feast is where life rejoices. Wandering in the arms of sunshine, Every soul feels the power of warmth.

THE SEASON OF BLAZING FLAMES

The sun burns like fire, scorching the earth's spine. Grass and trees sway, gilded in golden light. The air steams with the passion of summer, Like fireworks igniting every chest with fervor.

Distant mountains blush under the sunset's hue. Clouds flow with dreams of flaming intensity. The lake mirrors the crimson-tinted sky, A quiet hymn of the season's blazing fire.

The season's flames heat life to its core, Every ounce of passion ignites and soars. In this searing time, we chase and aspire, Fearless of burning, full of endless desire.

HEATWAVES EMBRACE THE EARTH

Rolling heat waves spread from the horizon. Their embrace awakens summer's brilliance. The earth, caressed by scorching hands, Burns with the fire of life in every grain of sand.

Distant shadows sway in the shimmering light, Cicadas sing memories of midsummer delight. Scorching breaths fill every heart, Bringing hope and fondness for what lies ahead.

The earth welcomes this passionate embrace, Absorbing sunlight to make seeds dance. Though the embrace burns, it is profoundly tender, Nurturing life in an unending cycle of splendor.

THE SUMMER DREAM OF THE LAKE

The lake's surface, a mirror, reflects the azure sky. A soft breeze stirs, leaving ripples behind. Sunlight scatters like golden shards, Lending the lake a dreamlike serenity that lingers.

Willow branches trail upon the water's face, Sketching the gentlest scenes of summer's grace. Fish leap and sprinkle crystalline drops, As if breaking the boundaries of this dreamscape.

The lake guards the secrets of summer, Each ripple whispers of hope and wonder. This summer dream, without an ending, Flows deeply within every heart.

THE FIERY PROMISE

The sun burns fiercely, its rays ablaze, A silent vow of life it conveys. Each ray pierces the darkness of despair, Paving a bright road to the future's care.

In deserts, it sparks glimmers of hope, Across oceans, it awakens waves to elope. With passion, it gilds the earth anew, Even in its heat, it remains steadfast and true.

This promise is buried in every beam of light, Guiding us through the maze of time's flight. A fiery pledge, like stars igniting a plain, Illuminates the boundless years ahead.

THE EVENING BREEZE'S WHISPER

The sunsets and the evening breeze arrive, Its cool touch soothes the restless sighs. It murmurs the day's weariness away, And gently delivers the night's calm sway.

It lifts the veil over the lake's surface, Singing a soft ode to nature's grace. It brushes treetops, rustling leaves' whispers, Smoothing the strings of every beating heart.

The evening breeze, though soft, carries deep affection, Bringing serenity as night takes possession. It's the tender moment after the sun's blaze, Whispering dreams of tomorrow's embrace.

THE RHAPSODY OF MIDSUMMER

The heat of midsummer rushes forth, Every ray of sunlight ignites the present's worth. Cicadas sing a symphony on high notes, While children's laughter dances under tree shadows.

The wind brushes through the grass, then swirls again, Carrying memories of fields and golden grain. Streams frolic joyfully between the stones, Telling tales of summer's enchanting tones.

This rhapsody is nature's celebration, Unrestrained, vibrant, and full of passion. In midsummer, we unleash our desires, Dancing endlessly with the blazing season's fire.

THE BURNING GREEN CANOPY

Beneath the trees, green flourishes like flames, Burning with life's magnificent acclaim. Sunlight pierces through the leaves seams, Painting a poetic interplay of light and dreams.

Cicadas sing their fervent tunes aloud, Turning the green canopy into a fiery crowd. The wind caresses the treetops, rustling whispers, Like a melody strummed on nature's strings.

Though ablaze, this green shade is intoxicating, Carrying summer's joy, embracing and creating. Each gaze at it cleanses the soul, The burning canopy renews life as a whole.

THE BLAZING YEARS

Youth burns brightly in the height of summer. Every dream is embraced by fiery fervor. Rushing steps, brimming with zeal, Painting life's canvas with unrestrained will.

Sweat flows, lighting up brilliance. Laughter blooms, setting the years ablaze. Every stride under the scorching sun, Writes the resolve of the young and dauntless.

The blazing years brook no hesitation, They shine as time's most radiant recollection. Though the sun's glare stings, steps press on, Life blooms miraculously in its fiery dawn.

THE SURGE OF LOVE

Heatwaves surge like tides of love, Embracing the earth with irresistible fire. Flowers bloom fiercely in the wind's caress, Hot as the emotions within each chest.

Every green leaf tells a story of affection. Every cicada's song echoes a heartfelt connection. Sunlight bears witness to these fervent hours, Illuminating every blazing moment of love.

Love surge washes away all indifference, Drenching every soul in its heated brilliance. In this searing season, love burns bright, Transforming into light, embracing all in its might.

THE SONG OF THE SCORCHING SUN

The scorching sun hangs high, the earth ablaze, Its song resounds with unyielding praise. The earth falls silent, listening in awe, To the sun's hymn of life's grandeur.

Sands shimmer like gold under its gaze, While waves echo its radiant refrain. Each ray carries power and aspiration, Igniting boundless dreams in every creation.

The song of the sun echoes across the skies, Singing life's primordial glory that never dies. Whether in the day or under the night's veil, Its melody flows through time's endless trail.

CLOUDS DYED RED WITH PASSION

The sunset ignites the edges of the sky. Clouds blaze like fire, burning deep inside. They carry the sun's final glow, Blending daylight's passion into a tender farewell.

Crimson hues paint the mountain peaks. The earth becomes a canvas of deep affection. In this moment, fervor and gentleness meet, Telling a tale of time's fleeting, regretless passage.

The glowing clouds fade into night embrace, But their warmth lingers, quietly ablaze. This sea of clouds dyed with passion, Is nature's confession of summer's fervent declaration.

FOOTPRINTS ON THE SAND

Footprints line the golden beach, Reflecting sunlight, stretching toward infinity. Each step carves a mark of the journey, A heartfelt trace of dreams pursued.

Waves kiss these fleeting poems of the moment, Carrying laughter, welcoming tomorrow. Steps, deep and shallow, speak of joy, As if summer follows in our stride.

The tide will softly erase the marks, But memories will forever dwell within. On the sand, we weave threads of hope, Our fiery youth singing in harmony with nature.

THE FIREWORKS OF MIDSUMMER

Fireworks bloom in the night sky, Igniting endless joy in the heart of midsummer. Each burst of light pierces the darkness, Leaving behind the most radiant moments of life.

Cheers erupt from the crowd below, Starlight and fireworks weave a canvas above. This fleeting yet eternal beauty, Adorns summer with a dazzling memory.

Under the night, heartbeats dance with brilliance, A fiery rhythm that ignites the soul. Though short-lived, the midsummer fireworks burn deep, Flaring with hope and an unforgotten passion.

THE FIERY CHASE

Fields stretch wide under the scorching sun. Shadows of runners elongate as they move. Every step carries the heat of youth, Every heart blazes with dreams aflame.

The wind brushes past, filled with vigor. The ground echoes the pulse of life. Sweat flows, bearing witness to the pursuit, As the fervent moment makes the spirit boil.

We chase in the direction of the sun, Toward a dazzling future of hope. This fiery chase, neither regretful nor restrained, It is life's most beautiful hymn.

THE MIDNIGHT STARS

The night is tranquil, stars scattered across the heavens, Like pearls embedded in the canvas of summer's sky. A gentle breeze brings a refreshing sigh, And every star seems to tell a tale of legends.

We gaze at the infinite universe, Releasing our dreams under the starlit expanse. These faint yet radiant lights, Guide the course toward unknown frontiers.

Starlight ignites midnight's musings, Allowing hope to pierce the barriers of darkness. Under the stars, we quietly wish, Awaiting the dawn's new promise.

HEATWAVES IN THE VALLEY

Heatwaves sweep through the valley, Rushing forth and igniting summer like a sea of fire. Each leaf gleams with dazzling light, Every breeze carries the scent of scorching fervor.

Streams flow merrily under the sun, Silver ribbons reflect the visage of summer. The cicadas' song fills the air with exuberance, Composing the symphony of life within the valley.

Though searing, the heat is full of passion, Endowing the valley with boundless vitality. In this fiery embrace, we pause to feel, Nature's burning essence and profound joy.

THE BLAZING BAGPIPE

The wind whistles across the hills, Playing a blazing bagpipe's melody. Each note leaps like a fiery spark, Burning in the deepest recesses of youth.

Shadows of trees sway, dancing with the breeze. Sunlight pierces through, painting a golden symphony. This bagpipe burns with the heat of flames, Igniting every untamed heart within.

Its blazing tune travels through the mountains, Echoing nature's ceaseless call. This bagpipe plays for the summer, An ode to life's fierce, unyielding passion.

THE PASSIONATE COAST

Waves wash the golden sands. Sunlight floods the passionate coast. Palm trees sway, their shadows gently drifting, Whispering the silent songs of the ocean breeze.

Distant sails dot the azure sky, Floating like dreams on the horizon's line. Footprints on the sand mark cherished memories, Telling tales of laughter and sincerity.

This Coast is a poem of fervor, Containing countless moments of heat. Amid the waves and sunlight, we wander, Savoring nature's infinite generosity.

LOVE AMID THE CICADAS' SONG

Cicadas sing their hymn of summer. Their melodies echo love's persistence. In dappled shadows, hands intertwine, Sunlight cloaked them in a fiery glow.

Each cicada's call is a proclamation of love. Every green leaf holds a vow. In this blazing moment, they embrace, Their hearts were aflame, pulsing as one.

Love blooms freely in the summer heat, Fearless of the sun, living for the now. The cicadas witness their boundless affection, Writing their story of love within summer's song.

CRIMSON LONGING

The sunset dyes the distant horizon red, Bringing longing, burning in every heart. Crimson light glows like an affectionate gaze, Crossing time, spilling endless dreams.

Each beam of light speaks of waiting, Each fading glow hides unspoken sorrow. This searing summer burns intensely, Igniting the embers of lingering devotion.

Crimson longing extends into the night, Dissolving into the depths of the stars. In this moment, the sky and soul entwine, Revealing endless yearning and memories divine.

CONFESSION OF A SUMMER NIGHT

A breeze brushes the tranquil lake, Summer Night is poetry-silent and deep. Stars scatter like murmured secrets, Telling tales of love from light-years afar.

Moonlight cloaks the night in gentle attire. Shadows of trees sway, revealing hidden hearts. Who whispers in the evening's embrace? Thrills soar with the song of a nightingale's grace.

Confessions of summer nights, etched among stars, Passionate yet serene, sincere and unbound. Though the breeze is light, it stirs the heart, Revealing that love has never drifted far.

SHADOWS UNDER THE SCORCHING SUN

The blazing sun scorches the vast earth. Shadows follow as loyal guardians in silence. Stretching and shrinking, always close by, They speak of sunlight's fervor without words.

Under this blazing radiance, we linger. Shadows march onward with our every step. Unfazed by the searing heat of the day, They mirror the shape of every dream we carry.

Even when sunlight blurs them into the haze, Shadows never indeed fade from our souls. Under the scorching sun, they remain quiet yet faithful, A steadfast presence on life's journey through.

YOUTH WRITTEN IN SWEAT

Beneath the sun, sweat drenches the fields. Stories of youth are written with passion. Each crystalline drop a burning testament, Telling of hard work and unyielding spirit.

Hands tightly grip the wheel of life, Steps carve out paths of fiery hope. Blazing days ignite boundless dreams, Sweat composes the anthem of endeavor.

Youth burns like a fierce and roaring fire, Each moment shines with brazen pride. In sweat, we find the essence of ourselves, Writing a life that never loses its color.

THE BURNING WHEAT FIELD

Golden wheat fields shimmer in the sunlight. Winds sweep through like dancing flames. Each stalk stands tall, like a lyrical ode, Singing of its love for the earth below.

Farmers wield scythes and the strength of toil, Harvesting hope, turning heat into sweetness. The burning wheat field holds more than sunlight, It celebrates life's homage to summer's grandeur.

Golden waves vanish into the distant breeze, Carrying the season's richness and grace. The burning wheat field transcends one summer, It's an eternal poem of life's endless cycles.

THE MOTH IN THE FLAME

The moth flies toward the fiery light, Ignoring the heat, yearning for brilliance. That flickering flame is its solemn faith-It is a brief life, yet it chooses to burn thoroughly.

Winds brush past the edge of the fire, Its wings carry fearless courage. In the flame, not just tragedy blooms, But also relentless pursuit without regret.

The moth melts into the fire, becoming dust, Illuminating the night and itself. The moth in the flame is life's hymn-Short but vivid, like a star's fleeting trail.

THE FRENZY OF MIDSUMMER

The summer air is scorching and thick. Every heart races with the heatwave's beat. Cicadas chant loudly like summer's drum, Stirring boundless fervor through the woods.

The blazing sun sets the sky ablaze, Every corner teems with vibrant life. On the shore, laughter and waves collide, A symphony of joy in midsummer's tide.

Midsummer is a festival of passion and bloom, Calling forth life's fearless devotion. In this frenzy, we freely let go, Leaving behind no regrets, only sparks of love.

DANCING IN THE HEATWAVE

Heatwaves ripple like an unseen melody. Steps move in rhythm under the sun. Each stride presses on the scorching ground, Marking life's fiery and passionate cadence.

Though shade is scarce, sweat flows like a song. Feet move lightly as if dancing in the breeze. Rising from the heat is not just warmth, But also the freedom and joy of the soul.

The dance doesn't stop, nor does summer pause, Creating fleeting moments of delight in the sun. Dancing in the heatwave, unafraid of the heat, For our hearts overflow with blazing happiness.

THE KISS IN THE FIRE

Flames roar, and heat waves churn. Two figures entwine in a burning embrace. Their kiss ignites the air between them, Scorching like sunlight, consuming the world.

Winds pass gently through their midst, Yet fail to steal the fire's ardent warmth. The kiss in the fire burns so intensely, It erases all doubt and hesitation.

Their love is as pure as the blazing flame. Though it may scorch, they have no regrets. In the fire, they hold each other tightly, Letting passion and life become eternal.

CHASING THE FOOTSTEPS OF SUMMER

The footsteps of summer are brisk and bold, Traversing mountains, scattering golden light. We follow its trail, hearts ablaze, Through meadows and shores teeming with fervor.

Wherever sunlight touches the earth, It leaves behind echoes of youthful strides. The footsteps of summer brim with zeal, Connecting every soul to their wildest dreams.

Though the sweltering air closes in, We march on, fearless in our pursuit. In the steps of summer, we leave our mark, Immortalizing every second as our own.

Part Four

AUTUMN: WHISPER OF ABUNDANCE

The richness and reflection of autumn symbolize mature emotions and the profound realizations of life.

YELLOW LEAVES DANCING IN THE WIND

Yellow leaves spin like sighs of time's lament, Swirling in the wind, a silent farewell. Each leaf tells a story of its own, Carrying autumn's gentleness and a trace of sorrow.

The branches grow sparse, standing alone in the vastness. The autumn breeze stirs, swaying memories of the past. The path paved with fallen leaves, where does it lead?Perhaps to the unknown or the depths of the heart.

Yellow leaves dance, whispering the season's secret, A continuation of life in another form. Whenever they whirl in the breeze, They are scripting autumn's poetry and painting its canvas.

AUTUMN WATERS AND ENDLESS SKIES

Autumn waters are clear, deep as a mirrored blue, Reflecting vast skies brushed with gentle hues. Ripples spread softly, like whispers of time, Binding distant mountains to clouds in silent rhyme.

A lone bird glides, sweeping through sky and water, Tracing a graceful arc in the vast, tranquil ether. The autumn breeze scatters its cool touch within, Carrying thoughts to a far and distant horizon.

Autumn waters speak no words yet brim with poetry. The endless skies reveal the earth's quiet serenity. In this canvas of sky meeting water, I see life's calm splendor and boundless wonder.

THE BOWING RICE STALKS

Golden rice stalks bow their heads low, Paying a resounding salute to the nurturing earth. Heavy gains, entirely like dreams, Bear the hope of countless sunrises.

The breeze brushes through, golden waves ripple, As if the earth smiles and sings softly. Farmers' faces beam with joy in their eyes, A satisfaction born of toil and sweet reward.

The bowing rice stalks are a gesture of harvest, A gentle confession to the cycle of seasons. On this land, silent fruit speaks, Of harmony between nature and humanity.

THE GOLDEN WOODS

The autumn woods are cloaked in golden hues. Sunlight filters down, dyeing every leaf. The breeze whispers, leaves rustle softly, As if murmuring secrets of the season's journey.

Squirrels dart, leaping from branch to branch, Seeking the hidden treasures of a year's harvest. A distant brook flows, crystal-clear as always, Composing autumn's symphony in the golden forest.

This golden world is nature's masterpiece, Each corner is a chapter penned by time itself. In the woods' embrace, I feel tranquility, As if everything returns to its pure, original form.

THE FRAGRANCE OF MEMORIES

Memories linger like a wisp of tea's aroma, Gently awakening old scenes from the depths of time. Laughter of childhood, mother's soft call, Ripple through the mind, warm and serene.

The autumn dusk resembles an aged photograph, Painting past moments in a warm glow. Each fallen leaf carries a fragment of a story, Fluttering down to stir the heart's buried longing.

The fragrance of memories needs no words, It exists in every deep breath we take. No matter how winding the road ahead, It will always be the sanctuary of our souls.

THE SUNSET'S AFTERGLOW

The sunset's afterglow spreads across the sky, Fiery clouds ignite the world with tender warmth. Mountains don robes of crimson and gold, Lakes reflect rippling waves of radiant light.

Herds return slowly along winding paths. Smoke rises, adding peace to the village air. A tapestry of light and shadow unfolds, As if time pauses in this dreamlike moment.

Though the sunset is beautiful, there's a trace of sorrow, As if bidding farewell to the day's tale. In the afterglow, I gaze at unfinished dreams, Waiting for tomorrow's sunrise to renew them.

THE SILENCE OF MOUNTAINS AND SEAS

Mountains and seas gaze at each other in silence. Their language is hidden in the wind and waves. The sea roars vast and boundless, The mountains stand tall, quiet against the heavens.

Sea breezes carry salty whispers to the peaks, Mountain streams pour their clear waters into the ocean. Their dialogue spans time immemorial, Telling stories of Earth's ancient legacy.

The silence of mountains and seas holds endless power, Revealing the depth and breadth of life. In the pause between mountain and ocean, One touches the eternal essence of nature.

THE EMOTIONS OF RED MAPLE

Red maples blaze, burning in the autumn sun. Each leaf is like a passionate confession. Their fiery hearts are written upon branches, Transforming the earth into a vibrant feast.

The wind stirs, scattering leaves in graceful descent, Like poetry sent from late autumn's hand. Each maple leaf bears fervent emotion, Each streak of red echoes yesterday's yearning.

The red maple's feelings run deep and true, Burning like flames in every heart they touch. They remind us to embrace life with fervor, To bloom brightly, even before winter's chill.

THE EMBERS OF LOVE

Love, once a blazing flame, burns out, Leaving only embers drifting in the wind. The fiery embrace and whispered words, Now fragments of time in ash-gray strands.

Yet embers are not entirely cold, They still hold the warmth of yesterday. In the quiet of the night, when revisited, They stir the heart with a faint quiver.

The embers of love are traces of the past, And a starting point to embrace life ahead. Passions burned need no regret, For they are the most beautiful moments of our lives.

STARLIGHT GUIDES THE LONELY BOAT

The vast night sky is scattered with starlight, Glistening across the river's tranquil surface. A lone boat drifts slowly on the rippling waves, Where water and sky merge in peaceful silence.

Lanterns aboard flicker like fireflies, Echoing the brilliance of stars above. Each star is a beacon, a guiding hand, Illuminating the boundless journey ahead.

Starlight accompanies the solitary boat, Offering the warmth of nature's solace. No matter where the river flows onward, The starlight is forever the voyager's home.

THE WHISPER OF AUTUMN WIND

The autumn wind gently sweeps, whispering like a song. Within the whispers, the stories of the season hide. It passes through the fields, taking away the green, Leaving behind a golden miracle across the land.

The leaves rustle, reciting the poetry of the time. The wind passes silently, yet deeply connected. Each gust is a messenger of time, Telling of past warmth and indifference.

The autumn wind whispers, delicate like a painting. It dyes the earth with soft twilight hues. The tenderness of these whispered words, It is the peace autumn leaves behind in the world.

GOLDEN REFLECTION

The mountain peak wears a golden robe, Autumn's contemplation ripples in the sunlight. The distant fields rise and fall like waves, A light breeze gently caresses, sweeping across golden depths.

The setting sun colors the outline of every leaf. A scroll unfolds between heaven and earth. In the golden world, one stands silently, Reflecting on the grace nature has bestowed.

Every golden hue tells a story, Of harvests and the poetic beauty of life. In this moment of peace, it melts into the heart, As warm and tranquil as gold itself.

THE LOVE SONG OF WITHERED LEAVES

Withered leaves fall, singing softly. Each turn a farewell, each twist a parting silhouette. They gently touch the earth, turning into soil, Completing the mission and instruction of the season.

The dusk light falls on the fallen leaves, As if lighting up their final brilliance. The wind is their accompanying melody, Rustling softly, like the echo of a heartbeat.

Though the leaves wither, they are filled with affection, Leaving love in the cycle of the seasons. This love song has no final chapter, For life blooms anew in the cycle of time.

THE AFTERGLOW IN THE MOUNTAINS

The afterglow of the setting sun fills the mountains, Dyeing every tree with warm red lines. The creek sparkles with golden light, Flowing with autumn's tranquility and sorrow.

The grass on the hillside bows in quiet thought, As if listening to the story of the setting sun. The distant smoke rises in the afterglow, Embracing the sky, telling the warmth of mankind.

The afterglow in the mountains is brief but far-reaching. It lights up the edge of twilight like a dream. The beauty of that moment cannot be put into words, It remains in the heart, becoming an eternal poem.

THE POEM OF AUTUMN DAYS

Autumn is the most dynamic brush of the poet, It writes chapters in golden and red hues. Each falling leaf is a rhyme, Every gentle breeze is a verse.

The light of the horizon is autumn's beginning, Soft yet carrying a hint of chill. The rice ears in the fields bow and sing, Telling the joy and generosity of the harvest.

The poem of autumn days hides in every corner, You just need to pause and listen quietly. In this vast and boundless season, Every scene is a continuation of poetic beauty.

AMBER MEMORIES

Amber seals the breath of time. The memories within it are as profound as autumn. Through its warm golden sheen, One can almost see the time that has passed, revived.

The sound of resin dropping still lingers, Nature carves it into eternity. Each drop of amber has a story to tell, Like an elegy written in the language of life.

Gently examining it in the autumn sunlight, The glow of amber brings a sense of peace. It reminds us to cherish the present moment, For every instant will become a cherished memory.

THOUGHTS IN THE WIND

The autumn wind rises, and thoughts drift away. Memories swirl in my mind like falling leaves. Those unfinished dreams and hopes, In the wind, become gentle sighs.

It caresses my face, bringing coolness, But awakens deep memories within. Every gust of wind carries endless stories, Each leaf tells a silent poem.

Thoughts in the wind guide my steps, Leading me toward a more distant home. In autumn's embrace, I wander, Letting thoughts and the wind dance together in the air.

THE SILENCE OF FROSTED MORNINGS

The frost covers the earth in the early morning, Dressing everything in a layer of sparkling white. The sky turns pale, the sunlight not yet risen, Only silence lingers in the air.

The birds' songs have not yet sounded. Cold light hangs from the branches. The breath carries the scent of winter, With each light step, a soft sound emerges.

This silence is like a wordless melody, Telling of nature's most profound tranquility. The beauty of the frosted morning is not in warmth, But in the eternal story, nurtured in stillness.

THE TALE OF AUTUMN LEAVES

Each autumn leaf has untold words. As it falls, it carries a thousand unspoken thoughts. Some express passionate confessions of life, Others bid a profound farewell to the past.

They dance with the wind, reluctant to part, As if lamenting the passing of time. Each leaf bears the weight of time, Reminding us of spring's first buds and vigor.

The tale of autumn leaves is a silent song. It falls, but its meaning is clear and profound. We bend down to pick up a fallen leaf, And we pick up a fragment of autumn's memory.

THE AUTUMN MELODY OF DISTANT MOUNTAINS

The distant mountains wear the rhythm of autumn. The misty clouds swirl, revealing a golden mystery. The layers of rolling hills rise and fall, As if chanting the story of nature.

The creek sings softly between the valleys, Accompanied by the echoes of the autumn wind. The mountains are painted with red leaves, Adding a vibrant touch to the autumn canvas.

The autumn melody of the distant mountains intoxicates. In that tranquility lies a deep emotion. Standing on the mountain peak, gazing at the painting, It seems one can see the grandeur and peace of life.

THE RETURNING SWALLOW

The swallow returns, soaring in the autumn sky, Carrying the warmth and longing of summer. It passes through winds and rain, crossing mountains, Finding its home under the blue sky and white clouds.

Each swallow is a messenger of hope, Carrying the scent of sunshine and soft wings. They dance in the air, gliding over the silence, Bringing a warm sound to the cold autumn days.

The returning swallow flies fearlessly as before, Singing its own song in the autumn breeze. With its wings, it draws a path of love, Making this autumn brighter because of them.

ORANGE AND YELLOW DREAMS

The orange-yellow sunset reflects upon the earth, Dyeing the horizon with its final tenderness. That glow is like the golden light in a dream, Bringing the coolness and depth of autumn.

In the fields, the curved rice ears hang low, Golden light shines upon every leaf. In this orange-yellow dream, I see, Time flows quietly, unspoken, and clear.

Every harvest is hidden in this dream. Every falling leaf records deep affection. The orange-yellow dream drifts to us, Bringing peace and profound memories.

THE HARVESTED FRUITS OF AUTUMN

The autumn wind rises, fruits hanging heavy on the branches, A gift the earth offers us in abundance. The weighty fruits shine brightly, Each one holds the blessing of the season.

The farmers' smiles are the song of the harvest, Their hands holding hopes full to the brim. Every grain of rice, every fruit, It is a testament to effort and time.

The harvested fruits are the heartbeat of the earth. Each bite of fruit tells a story. In this season, we taste together, This sweetness and power comes from nature itself.

THE JOURNEY OF THE SOLITARY GOOSE

The solitary goose soars, crossing the vast sky, Carrying the longing and sorrow of distant places. Its wings cut through the autumn expanse, Searching for a home in the wide-open sky.

Its silhouette is lonely but determined. Each flap of its wings is a cry from the soul. Flying south, flying toward a warm embrace, Carrying the cold autumn wind and silent song.

The solitary goose's journey is alone but filled with hope, It knows that home waits in the distance. Under the night sky, it passes through darkness, Embarking on its journey back home.

DEEP THOUGHT OF GOLDEN AUTUMN

In the golden autumn season, silent and profound, The earth sighs softly in the autumn breeze. Golden leaves fall across the mountain, They silently write the traces of time.

The fields are still, and the fruits are heavy. Each rice paddy is a poetic line of autumn. I quietly reflect on this land, Thoughts like wind drifting toward distant memories.

Deep thought in golden autumn brings peace and vastness. It feels as though I've found myself in the gold. My thoughts were no longer restless, In this tranquil autumn, I find my answers.

THE WITHERED BRANCHES UNDER MOONLIGHT

Moonlight spills over the withered branches, silver-white like frost. The night wind gently blows, causing the branches to sway. The withered leaves have long since been blown away, Only the bare branches remain, silently watching.

They no longer laugh but wait in solitude, As if waiting for the arrival of next year's spring. Under the moonlight, the withered branches speak in silence, They say nothing, yet hope is already planted in the heart.

The intertwining of withered branches and moonlight is a quiet painting. It is also the depth of life granted by time. In this moment, I see endless possibilities, Even withered branches have the strength for a future.

AUTUMN WATERS MEET THE ENDLESS SKY

The autumn waters are clear, meeting the endless sky. The mirror-like surface reflects the blue sky's image. The ripples stir, gently awakening the peace within, In this expanse of heaven and earth, all worries fade away.

The distant mountains are like ink, the distant sky like a dream. The autumn waters are silent, yet they convey strength in their stillness. In this painting, where water and sky are one, I see the vastness and depth of life.

The autumn waters and long sky intertwine. They tell the story of life's vastness and endlessness. At this moment, time seems to stand still, We and nature share this boundless and tranquil feeling.

THE SILENCE OF THE VALLEY

Deep in the valley, all is still. Only the wind gently brushes through the pine trees. The moss on the rocks is weathered by time, It seems to tell a thousand-year-old story.

There is no noise here, only silence. The heartbeat of the earth seems so clear. Everything grows in silence, Everything nurtures strength in quietude.

The silence of the valley is the sediment of life. It teaches us to find peace amidst the chaos. In this deep valley, I feel the vastness and tenderness of the universe.

THE DEEP AUTUMN SENTIMENT

The autumn air is thick with the scent of fruit. Yellow leaves fall, covering every inch of the earth. In the distance, the mountains whisper in the autumn breeze, Telling of the passing of time and its impermanence.

The rice ears in the fields bow their heads. The harvest season brings abundant joy. The autumn sun is like golden verses, Lighting the earth and warming the heart.

The deep autumn sentiment fills my thoughts. In this peaceful season, I immerse myself in nature's embrace, Feeling the most accurate breath of life.

THE PROMISE OF RED LEAVES

Red leaves like fire, burning in the embrace of autumn. They dance gently on the branches as if whispering. Each leaf is a promise, A vow to depart with the autumn wind, returning to the earth.

Their color is like a vow of love, Bright yet deep, carrying the warmth of time. The promise of the red leaves is unspoken, In each fall, leaving an eternal mark.

The autumn breeze gently brushes the leaves, slowly drifting down, A silent response to the cycle of the seasons. The red leaves remind us, no matter when, To bravely pursue the promises that belong to us.

THE RESIDUAL WARMTH OF AUTUMN NIGHTS

Autumn nights are like water, gently wrapping the earth. Moonlight spills upon the land, calm and peaceful. The residual warmth quietly spreads in the air, Carrying the afterglow of daylight, warming every heart.

It's the lingering tenderness after sunset. The soft caress still lingered in the dusk. The residual warmth of autumn nights is a quiet embrace, It makes one forget the cold, filling the heart with tranquility.

In this peaceful night, Every breath feels clearer. The residual warmth of autumn nights carries the fragrance of memories, Allowing us to feel the endless passage of life in the quiet moments.

FALLING LEAVES RETURNING TO THE ROOTS

The autumn wind and leaves flutter down like butterflies. They bid farewell to the branches and begin their journey. Falling leaves return to the roots, a call from the earth,

It is the law of nature: the return of life.

Each leaf has its resting place. They quietly transform into nourishment in the soil. Falling leaves returning to the roots is the most profound respect for life, A gentle farewell in the cycle of life.

No matter how bright and full of life they once were, Ultimately, they will merge into the earth's embrace. Falling leaves returning to the roots is a sense of belonging, A gratitude and remembrance of the past years.

THE ECHOES IN THE AUTUMN WIND

The autumn wind blows, carrying the whispers of leaves. They spin gently in the air, dancing in freedom. Each gust of wind is a low murmur of nature, Each falling leaf carries an echo.

The echoes in the autumn wind are songs of time, Soft yet profound, resonating within the heart. They speak of the changes and impermanence of the years, And in this moment, they offer us peace and comfort.

These echoes linger in the wind, Bringing a peaceful strength. The echoes in the autumn wind remind us, That amid all change, we should always maintain inner peace.

THE FRAGRANCE OF FRUITS

Fruits hang heavy, ripe, and complete, their enticing fragrance. The autumn orchard is filled with the scent of harvest. This is the earth's reward for the seeds it has sown, Every fruit hides autumn's secret within.

The fragrance of fruits is like a gift of time, It fills the air, sweet and rich. They are autumn's intentions, carrying hope, Each bite nourishes both the body and the soul.

The fruits of this season are plump and round. They stand as witnesses to hard work and patience. The fragrance of fruits always floats in the autumn wind, Making this season even more beautiful because of them.

THE LONG THOUGHTS OF AUTUMN DAYS

In the golden glow of autumn's dusk, the sunset's afterglow, At this moment, thoughts begin to spread. The light breeze blows, bringing a faint chill, In this tranquil time, my thoughts wander.

The long thoughts of autumn are reflections on the past, And hopes and waiting for the future. They are moments of quiet in the flow of time, A search for meaning deep within life.

Autumn, in long thoughts, is peaceful and far-reaching. It tells a silent poem with each falling leaf. In this season, I set my thoughts free, Letting them soar in the long thoughts of autumn.

WINTER: ECHOES OF SERENITY

The tranquility and vastness of winter represent the reflection of life and its eternal return

WHITE SNOW DRAPED OVER MOUNTAINS

White snow drapes the mountains; the sky is like a painting. The earth is silent, and the cold wind gently scatters. Thousands of mountains and rivers are sealed in white snow,

Adorned in silver, the years pass without a sound. The wind blows, the snow dances and the snowflakes fall, Like feathers or cotton, gently floating and overflowing. The mountains remain while time quietly passes,

The white snow falls, and time halts.

In this cold winter, The snowflakes carry away all the noise. White snow drapes the mountains, warmth fills the heart, The silent winter day is the most tranquil.

THOUGHTS IN THE COLD WIND

The cold wind blows; my heart moves with the wind. Thoughts from afar turn into the cold breeze. Each gust of wind carries a call, Each gust of wind carries longing. Your name drifts on the wind, I silently call your name in the cold. Your image scatters with the wind, But it remains in my heart.

The cold wind pierces, and thoughts are unyielding. On the winter night, there was endless loneliness. The cold wind brushes my face, warmth is hard to find, Longing like the wind sweeping through my heart.

STARS IN THE SILENT NIGHT

The night sky is tranquil, the starlight faint. A shooting star crosses the sky. In the silence, it flickers quietly, Bringing silent wishes and expectations. The stars seem to gaze, Each shooting star has a heart's desire. Through the darkness, it breaks the silence, Carrying away the reluctant brilliance.

In this silent night, I pray silently;I'm hoping the shooting star carries away my worries. Silent shooting stars, fleeting as a dream, Yet they illuminate the deepest desires in my heart.

THE FROZEN SEA

With the cold wave, the sea surface freezes. The blue ocean becomes still. Ice covers the surface, the sea solidifies, No longer raging, only silence remains. The sea breeze blows, the ice surface silent, Like a dream, freezing time. The sea's roar is sealed by ice, Only cold loneliness endures.

The Frozen Sea is a silent song, Telling of winter's ruthlessness and coldness. That sea, like a mirror, like ice, Holds endless loneliness and vastness.

A SONG OF THE COLD MOON

The cold moon hangs high, casting light on the snow. Its unmistakable glow is like water filling the earth. The moonlight sings softly, gently murmuring, Singing the most profound solitude of the winter night. The silver light falls on every inch, The cold moonlight is as cold as ice. The images under the moon slowly stretch, Night and moonlight weave into a dream.

The moon silently watches the horizon, Like a song, singing endless sorrow. Cold moon like a song, gently singing, Telling of the deepest longing on a winter night.

DISAPPEARING FOOTPRINTS

Lonely footprints are left in the snow. With each step, they quietly disappear in the cold. With the gentle breeze, they fade away, Like forgotten memories buried in the depths of time. Footprints grow distant in the white snow, Silent disappearance, never to be retrieved. Each step is a mark of the past, Each moment slips away in the river of time.

Those once-formed footprints have vanished, Leaving only the cold snowfield standing alone. They disappear in the cold wind, But the memories in the heart never fade.

THE WATCHFUL PINE

The cold wind pierces, and the pine tree stands firm. Through the years, it remains unyielding. Green and vibrant, it watches in the winter, Unafraid of the cold, silently guarding the earth. The wind and snow shape its branches, Still standing resiliently in the wind. The years sing the snow and wind sing, The pine tree hums quietly in the wind.

Each pine needle is the strength of life, Each snowstorm is their vow. The watchful pine grows in silence, In the cold winter, guarding the deepest hope.

THE BLOOM OF WINTER PLUM

Ice and snow cover, yet the plum blossoms alone. The cold wind is harsh, but it does not yield. In the winter chill, it quietly blooms, Like fire, lighting up the snow-white world. The fragrance of the plum flowers drifts into the cold air, The warmest scent in the winter. With its resilient stance, it announces to the world, No matter the cold, beauty can still bloom.

The winter plum blooms proudly alone in the snow. Its petals are like snow, pure and flawless. It is not afraid of the cold wind, nor the frost, Bringing the hope of spring in the cold winter.

THE FINALE OF LIFE

Time flows, and life grows old. Everything wilts in the baptism of time. Like falling leaves, they drift with the wind, Leaving only an empty memory. The finale of life is like a soft autumn breeze, Gradually silent, gradually calm. Every tear turns into a song in the wind, Every sigh becomes an echo of the wind.

The world in the finale is silent, But it is also the most real existence. In this last chapter of life, We learn to let go, to forgive.

THE OTHER SIDE OF THE STARRY SEA

The sky is vast, the sea of stars endless. In this boundless universe, my heart soars. On the far side, there are unknown dreams, Perhaps there is the home I've longed for. The starlight is like water scattered across the sky, Each star is a hope. They shine in the darkness, Guiding lost souls on their journey.

On the other side of the starry sea, there is a place, Where there is no loneliness, only light. I follow the stars in the distance, Searching for my piece of the starry sea.

WHISPERS OF FROST

Frost dances lightly, whispering gently, Silently covering every inch of the earth. In the stillness, it murmurs of cold, Telling of the ice and eternity in time. Each frost flower is a symbol of time, They quietly bloom in the night. The frozen air carries silent secrets, Whispers of frost softly sound in the ear.

They are silent yet convey profound meaning. Like the unspoken thoughts of winter, it is hard to express. In this frosty world, Every quiet night is filled with poetry.

LONELY SHADOW ON THE SNOWFIELD

The snowfield is vast, a blanket of white. A lonely shadow quietly moves forward. The wind blows gently, and snowflakes like feathers, Yet, it cannot carry away the loneliness within. In this silent world of white snow, Each step echoes in the cold. It is a journey of one, A silent and unspoken solitude, intense yet alone.

The snowfield is vast, the loneliness deep. Only the marks beneath the feet quietly fade. The lonely shadow floats in this snow, Like a passerby in the depths of time, never turning back.

In winter, the wind gently murmurs, Softly telling tales of the cold. Snowflakes drift, bringing peace, The air is filled with the scent of winter. Tree shadows stretch long, the cold wind howls, But deep within, there is warmth. The murmurs of winter are like a dream, like a vision, They softly tell us how to grow in the cold.

In this moment, tranquil and profound, Each falling snowflake is a note of the murmur. In the gentle winter, We hear the voice of time, distant and full of affection.

VIGIL OF THE WHITE NIGHT

The white night is like water, the stars like dreams. There is no darkness, only an endless soft glow. In this eternal light, I stand watch, With a warm hope in my heart. The silence of the white night surpasses time, Everything is still in the radiance. Never asleep, only waiting, Watching the distant shore, never reached.

The stars keep twinkling, reminding me. The white night no longer belongs to the night, It is the lighthouse of the soul, In the endless daylight,it lights the way forward.

THE FLOW OF THE ICE RIVER

The ice river flows slowly, time like a song. The cold water reflects the vastness of the sky. In this frozen world, Time seems frozen, standing still. The years flow like ice, silently passing, Each inch of ice is a mark of the past. The ice river is silent yet carries time, Allowing life to settle in the frozen world.

The ice river of the years has frozen all feelings, But it silently witnesses the strength of life. The water beneath the ice still flows, It is the song that time has not forgotten.

WINTER SUN'S GREETING

The winter sun shines through the clouds, gentle and calm. It spreads over the earth, bringing warmth. It is a greeting in the cold winter, Like a long-awaited, kind smile. The winter sun shines on the snow, sparkling like stars, Each beam carries the power of hope. It warms the cold heart, Like an unexpected tenderness in life.

The sunlight shines through the branches, reaching the heart. The winter sun's greeting is so simple yet profound. It makes the cold no longer seem lonely, Filling the winter with endless warmth.

CONTEMPLATION UNDER THE HOARFROST

Hoarfrost covers the branches, crystal-clear like a dream. The earth sleeps in the mist, quiet and soundless. In this world of ice and snow, I silently contemplate the truth of time. Each hoarfrost is a trace of time, They whisper secrets in the cold wind. The earth is silent, the air thick with frozen breath, I seek the answers in this soundless world.

The hoarfrost in contemplation sparkles with faint light, Like the philosophy of winter, deep and pure. In this quiet, snowy world, I learn silence, Learning to find inner peace in the cold.

MEMORIES ON THE SNOWFIELD

The snowfield is like blank paper covering the past. Each snowflake is a mark of time. On this silent snowfield, Memories gently fall, scattering in the wind. The snow buries the laughter of the past, The footsteps of the past are covered in ice and snow. But with each passing breeze, It seems to awaken those faint memories.

The memories of the snowfield are no longer clear, Yet they still flicker in the heart. They are the stories of winter, Forever preserved in the light touch of the snowflakes.

THE SILENT GLACIER

The glacier is silent, flowing quietly. Time sleeps in its embrace. A thousand years as one day, it remains unspoken, Its depth is like eternal silence. The heart of the glacier is cold and quiet, It holds all the past of the world. Silent, it quietly witnesses, The passage of time, the changes of the world.

The glacier needs no words; its existence, It is the most profound language. In its cold depths, It hides endless stories and time.

ECHOES OF THE WINTER NIGHT

The winter night is like water; the cold wind howls. Each gust carries the echoes of the past. It is the song of winter, low and distant, Resonating in the cold, never-ending. Each snowflake is a note in the echo, Falling gently, bearing the marks of time. On this silent winter night, I hear the voice of time drifting away.

The echoes of the winter night resonate in the heart. It is the melody of winter. It softly tells of life's impermanence, Yet, it brings a sense of peace in the cold.

THE SILENT PLAIN

The plain is quiet, covered in white snow. Not a sound, only the wind blowing. The earth is calm, time stands still, It is as if everything has frozen in this blank space. The silent plain, undisturbed by sound, Every inch of land breathes the cold. The wind gently sweeps by, the trees whisper, Yet the vast plain remains still.

In this silence, I hear my heartbeat. The silent plain gives me infinite space, Allowing me to meet myself and reflect.

THE BREATH OF FROZEN EARTH

The frozen earth is deep, covered in ice and snow, Its breath is like the silent depths of the sea. Every inch of land is frozen, Yet I can still feel its faint pulse. The breath of frozen earth carries the weight of time, Low and long, it echoes through the earth. Every ice crystal seems to tell a story, On this frozen earth, all life remains silent.

But the frozen earth continues to breathe. It is the heart of winter, quietly beating. The breath of frozen earth, carrying the essence of ice and snow, In the cold, it calls for new life.

THE DEEP AFFECTION OF FALLING SNOW

The falling snow is silent, as if gently sighing. It dances in the cold wind, carrying deep affection. Each snowflake is a tender feeling, Like the past falling softly in my heart. They gently cover every inch of the earth, Touching the land's wounds with icy hands. The deep affection of snow is hidden in its silent descent, It quietly speaks of love and longing in winter.

Each snowflake carries warm expectations. At the coldest moment, it quietly arrives. They melt the frozen heart, I hear a call of deep affection in the silent fall of snow.

A WINTER DAY'S SKETCH

The winter wind lightly brushes across the sky, Sketching with white snow-like paper.

The branches are withered, and the sky is silver. In the cold, the world seems like a silent canvas. Snowflakes swirl, outlining a quiet silhouette, Each snowflake is sketched with light strokes, They flutter down like accents of a pencil, In the winter day's sketch, everything is frozen.

The traces of frost outline the past. This season is like a silent painting. In the winter day's sketch, the colors are simple, Yet filled with tenderness and eternal stillness.

THE FROZEN VALLEY

The frozen valley is silent and still. All living things seem frozen in time. Mountains and rivers are silent, the earth's breath disappeared, The towering pines still stand but are swallowed by the cold, Every breath of air is frozen into frost. In the depths of the valley lies the secret of winter, It quietly waits for the return of spring.

That frozen world is deep and silent. No sound, only the whisper of the cold wind. The frozen valley waits for the moment it thaws, Where, in silence, new hope for life is nurtured.

THE FAREWELL OF FROSTED LEAVES

The frost-covered leaves sway gently in the cold wind. Their colors are no longer vibrant. Frost has covered the former greenness, They bid farewell to the last rays of sunlight. Each frosted leaf trembles, As if whispering goodbye to time. Their lives end in the frost, But in their fall, they leave an indelible mark.

The farewell of frosted leaves is like a silent vow, Softly echoing in the winter night. They will eventually return to the Earth, But that farewell will forever be etched in the heart.

A SILENT NIGHT

On a silent night, the stars hang low. The cold wind softly howls outside the window. Everything sleeps in the cold embrace, Only deep within the night does clarity remain. No bird calls, no insect sounds, Only the cold flows through the air. This silent night is deep and distant, It is as if entering another time and space, tranquil and soundless.

Moonlight spills on the snow like a dream. I feel the passage of time on this silent night. The silent night is so calm, In the stillness, I have a wordless conversation with the world.

THE LONELY BOAT IN THE SNOW

A lonely boat drifts on the frozen lake, Surrounded by endless snow and cold winds. The boat breaks the silence, leaving ripples, It searches for its way in the snow. Snowflakes gently fall, covering the boat, But the person on the ship is filled with loneliness. This boundless snowfield has no human sound, Only the lone boat dances with the wind and snow, solitary yet steadfast.

The lonely boat is like a drifting soul. On the cold night, it keeps moving forward. Even if there are no bright lights ahead, It must find its way in the snow.

COLD DREAMS

Cold dreams are like a sleeping lake, Bottomless and chilling. In the dream, everything is a frosty scene, Frozen time, carrying a biting air. Each step is on the ice, The echo is clear but hollow. Cold dreams overshadow the soul, Making one lost in endless cold.

But at the end of the dream, There is a warmth like spring, Waking the sleeping soul, Letting light emerge from the cold dreams.

THE WINTER WIND'S ELEGY

The winter wind is like a song, blowing over the barren earth. It hums softly, filled with endless sorrow. Each gust of wind is a funeral song, Telling of the cruel passage of time and regret. It passes through withered branches, ice, and snow, In the cold, it sounds like the horn of solitude. The elegy of the winter wind has no tears, only chill, It sings of parting, of time's wordless farewell.

On this quiet winter day, The winter wind continues its low song, distant and sorrowful. It carries all this sadness away, Leaving behind a wordless echo, deep and long.

THE DEEP SLUMBER OF BITTER WINTER

The deep slumber of bitter winter, snow covering the earth, All things sleep in the cold embrace. The winter sky is cold and far-reaching, It gently closes its eyes, entering a silent slumber. Snowflakes fall, covering mountains and rivers, The trees still stand as if guarding this stillness. The deep slumber of bitter winter has no sound, only peace, It makes everything blurry and distant.

In this deep sleep, The world seems to have entered an endless winter. The slumber of bitter winter is waiting, Waiting for the spring sunlight to awaken gently.

SNOW TRACES UNDER THE MOONLIGHT

Moonlight pours down; the snow is like a mirror. Every step leaves a deep imprint on the white snow. Snow traces shine brightly under the moonlight, They tell a silent story, long and gentle. Moonlight-like water filters through the shadows of trees, Snow traces spread under the light, softly speaking. Each footprint is a memory, The path walked in winter is tranquil and profound.

The snow traces under the moonlight are eternal. They witness every bit of the past. On this snowfield, Every trace is a mark of time, precious and undying.

THE WHISPER OF THE NORTH WIND

The north wind whispers in the night sky, Carrying cold, crossing the earth. Each gust of wind is a whisper, It quietly tells secrets on the winter night. The north wind doesn't speak, yet it has endless words, It passes through treetops, through rooftops. Its voice is soft yet powerful, Bringing endless cold in this silent night.

The whisper of the north wind seems to remind us, The cold is not to be feared; what is feared is forgetfulness. It blows through every corner, Leaving a silent echo, carrying traces of time.

STARLIGHT ON A SNOWY NIGHT

The snowy night is like a painting; the stars twinkle, White snow and stars weave together. The starlight in the sky is cold and bright, Falling on the snow like fragments of a dream. Snowflakes dance lightly, the starlight reflects, Each snowflake is a reflection of the starry sky. On this peaceful, snowy night, The starlight and snowflakes are together, telling the story of winter.

The starlight on the snowy night is gentle and poetic.

ETERNITY IN ICE AND SNOW

Ice and snow blanket the earth, a vast expanse of white. The cold wind blows, carrying fragments of time's flight. All sinks into silence beneath the frozen veil, As if stepping into eternity's still, timeless tale.

Snowflakes drift down like the footprints of time, Dancing lightly in the chill, then vanishing in rhyme. Each snowflake bears a promise, fragile yet profound, A pledge of existence, an echo of life unbound.

Eternity in ice and snow is not a silent freeze, But a force of life gathering strength beneath the frigid seas. It hides within the smile of each delicate flake, Quietly budding in frost, awaiting spring's wake.

EPILOGUE: EMOTIONS AND THE MOUNTAINS AND SEAS

Summarizes the themes of the four seasons, elevates the core meaning of the collection, and looks forward to eternity

THE EVERLASTING MOUNTAINS AND SEAS

Mountains stretch far, the sky endless. Time flows on, but still, the heart remains steady. Pines stand tall, their roots deep like a dream, Waves crash upon the shore, each one whispering its story.

A thousand years before, a thousand years to come, The earth speaks no words, yet the world endures. Wind and sand sweep by, leaving traces, The sea surges forward, washing away sorrow.

Mountains high, rivers long, when will they cease?Time speaks in silence; only eternity understands. Unmoved by worldly matters, untouched by dust, The mountains and seas remain, and the heart moves with the wind.

THE FAREWELL OF THE TIDES

Tides rise and fall; the sea breeze hums. Each farewell is a new beginning. Waves surge forward, carrying yesterday away, Then, gently return, burying the marks of the past.

In the heart, a farewell drifts away like the tide, Silent yet full of deep affection. Every approach is a goodbye, Every departure is a chance for reunion.

The tide speaks not; the shore is silent. Their farewells never cease. In this endless cycle, The tide sings like a song of goodbyes and hope.

THE CYCLE OF THE SEASONS

Spring breeze caresses the face; flowers bloom like dreams. Summer rain falls in abundance, green and thriving. Autumn leaves fall, the ground covered in gold, Winter snow dances lightly, the earth dressed in silver.

Seasons change year after year, Like the rise and fall of life and its slow settling. Spring warmth and blossoms, the summer heat unbearable, Autumn harvests and winter's rest, everything is natural.

Each season is a cycle, Each moment is a rebirth. The steps of the seasons never stop, They tell us that time is eternal.

RETURNING TO SILENCE

The bustling has gone, and the clamor fades. The soul returns to silence, tranquil like water. All things fall silent, time moves on,

The sounds of the world gradually disappear.

Night falls, and the stars shine bright. Yet within, there is still peace. All troubles return to dust, Only calm remains in the depths of time.

Silence is not lonely, It is the serenity and contentment within. Returning to silence, the heart is free, No matter how vast the world, it no longer fears solitude.

THE ETERNITY OF EMOTIONS

Emotions, like the wind, gently brush the heart. Tender gazes etched within. It needs no words, no proof, A deep affection is the eternal presence.

Time hurries on, yet love never leaves. It lives on in every fleeting moment. No matter how time flows, Emotions remain deeply buried.

It is the morning light, the stars at night, A watchful heart, never fading. The eternity of emotions is not about never changing, But about the light that never dies, after the storm.